CW00821905

Messages

Ascended 1

Germain

A Workbook of Spiritual Steps to Grow Your Soul

"This book is unique as it requires effort on the part of you, the reader. This is a book for those on a path to realizing their own being and who they may become. We open doors for you. This requires action on your part. This is not a relaxing story to numb the body and mind, but a workbook demanding full participation." Saint Germain

Jane Halliwell Green

DEDICATION

With deep love and gratitude, I dedicate this book to my Heavenly
Father, Saint Germain, Saint Brigid of Ireland, Archangel Raphael,
Jesus, and my personal guides and angels. I am grateful to my
teachers in both the physical and invisible worlds. These teachers
make it possible for me to serve those individuals who seek out my
services.

iii

CONTENTS

Dedication   iv

Preface   Pg#1

1   Love, Fear and Forgiveness   Pg#5

2   The Soul's Journey   Pg#14

3   The World   Pg#18

4   Family   Pg#28

5   Body, Mind, Soul   Pg#36

6   Angels, Guides, Orbs   Pg#48

7   Spiritual Gifts   Pg#55

8   Universal Symbols   Pg#59

9   Death, Past Lives   Pg#74

10   Dreams   Pg#82

11   Life On other Worlds   Pg#85

12   Saint Germain   Pg#87

13   Final Words   Pg#90

ACKNOWLEDGMENTS

My thanks to my husband Don, my daughter Kate Senger, and my sister Susan Knade for their assistance in reading and editing the book. Deep appreciation for my mentor and friend, Robin Rice for her encouragement and wisdom concerning all aspects of spiritual work. I am grateful to Philip Burley for his outside validation of my connection with the Ascended Master, Saint Germain. Special thanks to Emily Knade for designing the cover of this book.

Preface

I am pleased to share this book with you. It all started one morning in July of 2013 when I was awakened by the sound of a loud voice that said, "Arise, Arise and hear the clarion call for one and for all." I grabbed my husband who had been fast asleep and shouted, "Someone must be in the house." The house however, was quiet. As I drank my morning coffee I realized that a spirit was trying to get my attention.

I have been able to hear spirit voices since I was a little girl. When I was 13 I asked my grandmother, who had immigrated to the United States and was a devout Roman Catholic, to teach me how to read the cards. She was trained by the gypsies who lived on her family's farm in Ireland. My large Irish family was surprised when she agreed to teach me to read the cards as it had been kept a secret, even from her own children. She told the family that I had the gift of "sight," like her, and that is why she agreed to teach me.

She spent many hours with me as I practiced her card reading techniques. Her method used a regular pack of cards. She recited an unusual meditation to select the cards and this was taught to me. The cards were divided into seven piles and each one had a special meaning. The suits and numbers were important as well as the order in which they came up in the reading. I became quite popular with my friends once they learned I could tell their fortunes! One day while doing a reading I heard a deep male voice with an accent speak to me. I thought there was something wrong with me. I visited my grandmother and asked her what this was all about. Her response was that I was simply hearing my angels. After that moment, most of my readings were channeled. Channeling is the act of serving as a medium through which a spirit guide communicates with a living person. This means that instead of interpreting the face value of the cards, I relayed the information I was hearing from my spirit guide instead. In order to channel, one must hear spirit. This is referred to as clairaudience, which means "clear hearing," and is a spiritual gift I have had since childhood.

As I matured, I also found myself able to see clairvoyantly and feel, energetically, the presence of spirit. The morning I was awakened so abruptly by Saint Germain was the culmination of many years of spiritual study and working with spirit guides. These guides have always been my greatest teachers.

On that morning in July, 2013 I sat quietly and placed myself in a deep state of relaxation to learn which spirit was trying to get my attention. I asked for the spirit to speak to me again. In my meditative state I was taken to a place on a high cliff overlooking the ocean. I could see myself walking up the steep steps to a cathedral with no roof. Standing at the entrance was a gentleman dressed in beautiful robes. He greeted me and told me he was the Ascended Master Saint Germain. He said we would work together, and that would include writing this workbook.

Saint Germain was very specific that this would be a work book. Almost every chapter requires your participation in order to grow spiritually. I have tried to transcribe his words as accurately as possible with minimal editing. Some of the words are capitalized because I used an automated software program. The caps came out without any input from me. I accepted this as a sign and left them unedited.

The book contains an energetic imprint. As you work through the exercises, your energy will begin to shift. This will affect the way you look at everything in your life. Saint Germain said this to me early in our work together: "the world as you know it is a place of work, study; -- self – directed and organized by the Guides and Angels who teach you. This is a program of study. You and your classmates change as the lessons are mastered. Achieving mastery qualifies one to move into a higher realm of being once the body has died. This is the ultimate goal." Saint Germain defines mastery as one who has reached a full understanding of his or her connection to love all other beings in and through the father. This curriculum is designed to push you forwards in your understanding of your highest purpose here on earth. The answer to your question, "why was I put on this earth and for what reason," will become clear. This is why we have written a workbook with a deeper purpose. In our classroom, it will be a powerful addition to the support of your own personal guides.

This manuscript is almost entirely channeled, and is arranged in a question and answer format. Q is a question asked by myself, and SG is Saint Germain's response. Other spirits will participate as well, such as Saint Brigid. Their names will be spelled completely. Most chapters will end with a lesson which requires your action. I suggest that you start a journal to accompany this book. In this way you will have a record of your journey through this amazing material.

Q-I told Saint Germain that I loved the idea of a class. I asked, are there grades?

SG- No, not as you are accustomed to. The grading is done by one self and the grade reflects the diligent adherence to the reading and contemplation of the content of each lesson. This book is a series of lessons. Each may be guided by Masters and your personal guides. I promise you that this effort will change your life in very distinct and noticeable ways.

Note-Many of the questions were asked by me because of my curiosity. I hope they answer some of you own questions. I feel blessed to share this with you and to be able to help so many people through my connection with spirit. Thank you for embarking on this fascinating journey with me and Saint Germain.

"This book is unique as it requires effort on the part of you, the reader. This is a book for those on a path to realizing their own being and who they may

become. We open doors for you. This requires action on your part. This is not a relaxing story to numb the body and mind, but a workbook demanding full participation." St. Germain

CHAPTER 1
LOVE

Today I will teach you the meaning of love – not love the human way but love from a universal perspective. Every molecule has the spark of life; every tree is living and breathing. Every creature needs to be recognized. Love knows this on a deep cellular level. Human beings expect not to be loved. They are deprived and cut off from all that there is. - St. Germain

Q-What is love?

SG-You are love. Your friends and enemies are also love. This is fundamental and must be understood before a soul graduates to a higher level of understanding and becomes a leader in spiritual armor. Love is universal in both the physical and spiritual dimensions. Just as it is not always practiced in your world, the same is true here. If love is practiced while within a physical body, it can be taken to the non-physical words when you die. Love is supreme. Nothing reins above it. To love is beyond the understanding of any human being. To even get close to this understanding as a physical being is a miraculous thing.

Q-How can we help people elevate their ability to love others?

SG-Always remember that each and every BEING is linked together with the Father. No one stands alone. Love is what is missing in most people's lives. This must be repeated in many ways. Never hesitate to say I love you. Light comes to those who practice the greatest of all gifts—love.

Love does not flourish without relationship. Those who are detached from relationship with others are separated from themselves. These souls must be brought into the circle of connection.

Q- How can you treat someone you love in an unloving way?

SG-All sentient beings on the physical plain perform the dance choreographed before the soul enters human form.

Note-In this statement, Saint Germain is referring to the careful planning that takes place before we are re-born into the physical world. There is additional information about this process in other chapters.

Q-Teaching love is hard. How does one do this?

SG-Each family carry's a burden of pain. No matter where they go to escape the pain, the fear is carried also. The pain body is like a rock tied around your heart. As one travels to a new place, changes one's livelihood, makes new friends, the pain and fear also follow. Take on love. Love the fear. Love needs pain. Love solves all problems and the world needs this medicine.

Q-Can you say more about love needing pain?

SG-All love, like anything else has an opposite does it not? To appreciate the energy of love one must also experience its opposite. Most relationships require both. Those who choose to work with the pain will eventually fall back into love. Those in relationship that reject the pain will leave the relationship.

Q-Do most relationships end this way?

SG-Yes, the pain is the test and one may pass or fail.

Q-I left a painful relationship but I had resolved the issues and left on a level of love for my partner. Did I fail?

SG-No, this was the test. Despite the departure, you had resolved the relationship on the level of love, and so you passed.

Q-How can you make someone love? How is a deep-seated emotion changed?

SG-Use love as a bullet in a gun. Shoot it at everyone. Send it like a cannon pumping out balls of love. Just as prayer, which is love, can heal and effect change, love balls have power beyond your current understanding. I will send one to you now.

I felt a powerful rush of warm air strike my body while channeling this information.

SG-Love is all there is. The rest are only tools to teach and bring all to love. Every hurdle in life will be a call to love. Every divorce, fight, mean thought, or crime, must lead to love. There is nothing else, and so this is the most important teaching as we begin to talk about the things of your world.

Q-Can love be realized without forgiveness?

SG-This is an excellent question and the answer of course, is no. Forgiveness always precedes love. Dysfunctions in the relationship will block love from prospering. Forgiveness precedes peace and then a path opens up to love.

Q – How do we practice love?

SG- I will provide instructions. Practice saying, I love you to every person you meet. Quietly, inside your mind say a prayer – I am a Holy Spirit and everyone I see is pure love. Pray, and those difficult people will be easier to live with.

Q-Can the church help people be more loving?

SG-The organized church is not able to help many people. Organized religion, as you know, is more of a business. Please understand that those of you willing to participate in this exercise will increase one's understanding of their own being. Here in the spiritual realms we would like you to know that your participation is acknowledged by us.

Note – I recommend using a separate journal to work through the exercises. Some involve writing and others require images and words.

Lesson: Practicing Love: Part 1

1. List all the people you love deeply without conditions.

2. List all those individuals you love, or think you love, but with some conditions.

3. List those you do not love and the reason why.

4. List all people you hate.

Lesson: Practicing Love: Part 2

Take lists 1, 2 and 3 and next to each person rank the degree to which you love each one with 1% being the lowest and 100% the highest.

Lesson: Practicing Love: Part 3

1. Separate lists 2 and 3 into those in the 50% and above category and those below 50 %.
2. Do the same for list #4.
3. Work from the bottom up: 1% to 100%

Take the 4th list and beside each name write a positive sentence about each person. Our goal is to move at least half of this list up to the 3rd level. Repeat this with all other lists.

Practicing Love and Building relationships: Part 4

List the names of all close family and friends. Create a diagram of your connections. Color all the love connections in pink.

Each soul must have deep and abiding connections at the most holy level. The greater the number of these relationships, the higher ones knowledge of his/her place in the Universal matrix.

Q- What if someone is alone?

SG-Always reach out to those who swim alone in the sea of connection. Love them and bring them into your symbolic circle. Find them and link them to others.

Q-So no man or woman should stand alone?

SG-This is the lesson. Love is the greatest lesson and once it is mastered all other issues in life are resolved.

Note- One of the most heartwarming things is to approach someone and extend your hand to welcome them. As they reach out to shake your hand, place your left hand on top of the other two hands. At the same time, smile warmly, look into their eyes and to yourself say, "I love you," and mean it. Do not release their hand immediately, but continue saying to them I love you. Let it sink in. You will be amazed by the reaction. If we all spread love to even one person a day what a wonderful world we will create!

Prayer of Love:

Blessed are you who love. Love is the ultimate experience in this life of physicality and spirit. Love will provide you with the riches of the universe, unlike the artificial riches many strive for. Practice true and deep soul love-soul love at the deepest level of your being. Love embraces all. Love is beyond the understanding of the human part of you. To embrace and know it at its deepest level, one must first tap into the spirit which is who you really are. Pray to understand, and practice loving those you believe do not deserve it. All deserve love. All respond to love. Love is the most potent medicine in existence. We challenge you to use this power to change your world. Do not be skeptical until it is tried. To change your situation requires that you be loving and nothing less.

Fear

SG-There is a world of fear. It is humankind's attempt to control. Fear is deeply planted in America. We do not want you or others in human existence to live with such a thing.

Q- How can this be changed? The world seems very unstable now?

SG-Fear is like a mosquito—is it not? It bites and spreads disease. It multiplies and leaves welts on the body.

I responded that is an excellent metaphor.

SG-Each person must battle this emotion when inhabiting a physical body. None can escape. One must go within to gain control. Fear has always been an opponent of love. Send love to the fear. Surround it with the pink light of love. Nurture the fear. Do not try to wipe it away as it will emerge stronger. Always place it in the light of love. Change creates fear for many people but this is what life is all about. Nothing ever stays the same. One must ride the waves of change.

Q-How do we let go and allow change?

SG-One gets stuck working through the dense energy of the physical world and as you know one needs to feels safe. There is no safe place. Life is a challenge and a program. Life on earth was never meant to be easy. All souls are aware of this before birth.

Forgiveness and Harmony

There can be no harmony without forgiveness- Saint Germain

St. Brigid - I speak to you of the universal principle of harmony, forgiveness, and everlasting love. These are the basics of all life. To hold this in the highest level of understanding and love is the ultimate goal of all sentient beings. The word forgiveness has deeper vibration and when it is spoken brings healing to the soul. We ask that the words forgiveness, love, and harmony are combined in a way that holds energy which may be sent to others as well as heal the sender. Forgiveness will create harmony in all efforts to reach the spiritual peak, and love will be sent to all who hear these powerful words. They shall receive this energy.

Q-How do we use these words?

Saint Brigid- "Pray, Holy Father I create harmony in my life and that of others by sending forgiveness and love to them. I see the word forgiveness become light and pulsate out to the world around me. I forgive the world and all beings in it, and as they forgive their world, the light of forgiveness permeates the field and creates harmony. This perpetuates the greatest gift of all – universal love."

Q-How can this be expressed in a concrete way?

SG-The responsible soul will never hold onto a painful drama and not release it to the light.

 I commented that it was like drinking poison and expecting the other person to die.

Prayer of Forgiveness:

Holy Father we bless all souls in or out of the physical body who practice the art of forgiveness. Nothing is important without complete adherence to this foundation of spiritual growth. Be forgiving, practice forgiveness, and forgive anything that hurts or is

11

thrown outward to change the energy field from light to dark. Send balls of light filled with love to those who need this special energy. Harmony requires forgiveness--life in balance--time placed in its proper perspective—life moving smoothly in both the inner and outer realms, knowing there is a grand plan.

SG- Harmony is missing in the world, and it's opposite—discordance is the supreme ruler in our society. Nature represents the harmonious movement of sea and sky, earth and water. Fear, anxiety, television violence are not harmonious things. Those who have re-connected with their source can experience harmony in a world of discord, but if one has lost this connection they are out of balance.

Saint Germain shows me a picture of a person going through their day having to push life-size marbles around in order to get anywhere. These huge objects obstruct sight and make movement difficult.

SG-Your lives should be easier than this. Light beings are standing next to you and their only desire is to serve with the goal of helping you to reach the highest potential for your soul.

Grace

Note- In the Bible, Grace is defined as a gift from God to all mankind. Saint Germain indicates that Grace is earned.

SG- Grace follows good actions. Loving all beings and practicing forgiveness brings forth its power. Grace is a powerful word and the soul who is clothed in its power is clearly felt and noticed by others. Grace is like flying on the wings of a great white bird—soaring through life with a sure knowledge that only a spiritual view of the world matters. Old souls have earned grace. Young souls carry the uncomfortable "static" associated with self (ego). The focus on the "me" with its wants and needs does not lead to grace.

One who uses boundaries in a negative way is not a candidate for Grace. A boundary can be a positive thing if one uses it to restrict those with negative energies from crossing the line. A boundary can also be negative if one uses it to shield themselves from the good and loving behavior of others. One is protective, and the other designed to separate.

Once grace is earned it can also be lost. This happens when a soul forgets their connection to all other sentient beings under the umbrella of love.

Prayer for Grace

Holy Father, we bless those who have earned grace through their love of all other sentient beings. Love, kindness and forgiveness, paired with the knowledge of the energy connection between oneself and others will result in the gift of Grace. Know that when you wear the gift of grace it draws love toward you as well.

Prayer to connect with the divine:

I am the Divine working through me. I am harmony through connection with the force of the universal God.

SG- I end this discussion on another harmonious note that all mankind will be lifted up by remembering the connection binding you to the earth, other beings, and to spirit.

CHAPTER 2

THE SOULS JOURNEY

We pray, Holy Father, to be blessed every time we embrace or hold hands with another soul. Touch everyone you can. Hold the hand and extend love, compassion, physical support, or what they may require from you at this moment. See your friends, family, neighbors, and associates as family and take responsibility for them. Give love and receive love. Pass love around. This is the meaning of your life – no other word carries the power of love except love. Be and live love. Amen.

As mentioned previously in the preface of the book, this book is to give you a better understanding of your soul's place in the univese. There is a special energetic signature coded into this written material, and the ownership of the book brings you energy as well as knowledge.

SG -We begin today by speaking of the soul's journey upwards to a better understanding of who they are and what their purpose is on planet Earth. Your soul is the part of you that exists eternally. The body is finite. The body is supported by the soul, and once the soul departs, it is reduced to ashes.

Once a soul has entered the physical realm, even as babies, it has been given a workbook of sorts. This workbook is a selection of things they must do in this life.

Q-So you are saying that we come to this planet with things that we have to do; however, most people forget they have a list of tasks?

SG-This is a very good question. As you live your life, and this is very short in spiritual terms, you are prompted to remember your lessons for this body and mind. As we have discussed before, each soul has been gifted with a guide and an Angel who have the larger purpose of their plan in mind and will bring forth the remembrance of the lessons.

Q-How do we help the readers of this book remember some of these lessons?

SG-Some are ready to remember and must make a list of all the turning points in the current life. After each event the resulting action should be disclosed. This exercise will bring forth a powerful remembrance, and shift the energy to a new level.

Q-To clarify, we should make a list of all the moments that seem to be very important for us in our life so far. Possible events might be a transition from one marriage to another, the birth of a child, or when someone new is introduced and there exists a feeling that this may be the beginning of an important relationship. Then we should list the resulting actions and feelings. Am I correct?

SG-Yes, for those who are ready to understand their purpose this exercise will be powerful.

Q-Does an individual have to be in a difficult situation like a car accident, or in some type of deep pain to recognize angelic encounters? In other words, can we see signs outside of these big moments?

SG-You ask a very good question. We expand and embellish this information. Remember, that signs can be very personal and only important to the person who recognizes them. In general, all life changes are opportunities to remember the book of life tasks. All new souls emerging and joining the life force are here for a reason. So all heartache, calls for courage, lost opportunities, major spiritual breakthroughs or chance encounters show that spirit is present. These are signs and clues to the life plan.

Note- This book of Life Tasks is known as the Akashic Record. It contains the record of all our past lives, including the goals established for the current life-time. There is more about this topic in Chapter 9.

Q-The United States is a particularly difficult place to live. How do people recognize the signs when they are so busy and caught up with their own lives?

SG- Yes, this is a concern, but also a part of the soul's journey. The choice of where you live is your choice, and this culture brings its own challenges. Other countries on the planet teach other lessons.

Q-So we opt in to the chatter and the culture?

SG-Yes everything is a personal choice.

Pray that I be placed in remembrance of the directional markers you have given me in my lifetime here on earth. Please make these markers visible to me, so that I might grow closer to my true spiritual being. As I explore who I really am, my soul will extend beyond its original blueprint.

Q-So the original blueprint can be bypassed if one wants to reach higher?

SG- Yes, in that certain lessons may be achieved quicker than originally planned.

Q-Is this intricately planned and not spontaneous?

SG–This is a grand plan and one which brings spontaneity as well. All plans may be modified, neglected, or adopted by the soul's desire.

Q- How does this plan happen? Is there a Council of Elders or is it more sophisticated than that?

SG – A business plan is created by a group including you. All souls have a team – Council – soul teachers that work out the particulars with the assistance of you.

Q-It sounds like there is a lot of counseling?

SG–Yes but with great love and compassion for the plan. A plan may be quite challenging. All is done with the greatest love, and all souls understand the work ahead.

Note- In our soul's journey in the physical world there are very few accidents. All proceeds based on a divine plan. To better see your plan, try the exercise that follows.

Exercise

Make a list of all the moments that stand out as very important and possibly turning points in your life so far.

Next to each event list both the emotion associated with the event and the action taken.

When these events are seen from the current moment, the greater spiritual plan begins to be seen.

CHAPTER 3

THE WORLD

This world in which you reside is like a plastic toy wrapped up in paper that crinkles and makes noise. This represents the world in suffocation and separate from what is real. - Saint Germain.

Understanding Physical and Spiritual Worlds

Q-Where is the location of the spiritual realm? Is it in the same space as the physical dimension?

SG-All realms exist simultaneously in the same location. No world as we know it here has a location.

He asked me if I understood that and I answered no, I wasn't sure.

SG-All spirit realms are those of higher vibration and dimension and do not take up space. Spirit is everywhere and nowhere you might say.

St. Germain allowed Jesus to step forward to describe this further Jesus said the following:

Jesus-I can describe this child as the layers of an onion. As I peel off the outer layers which are the protective coat we go deeper into the center of the plant. The heart of the dimension in which we sit now is the center of the onion – not above, or around it. It is the inward, not the outward direction. At the center of the onion there exists energy to create and support the growth of the plant. As you exist in the physical dimension so do the inner realms which do not have form but support you and the others now present in physicality.

I repeated the message in my own words by saying, "The spirit is the core and this is the real fuel and the real substance, and the real seed continuing to grow and nurture new plants."

SG- I would like to talk about the issues of the material world from a spiritual standpoint. The materialism of your world is not all that there is. There is a non-material substance which surrounds and manages to affect the physical.

Q-Are you referring to energy?

SG-Yes and no – all things are energy. The spiritual realm is all energy and although you may think as you stand on this floor that it is solid, it is not.

 Note-This last sentence is not about standing on earth, but is about standing in front of St. Germain in the spiritual realm. I see him clairvoyantly in a setting that looks real.

SG-The same is true for all of our earthly surroundings. The object looks solid, but when taken to the smallest particle it is only energy. There is nothing in your world that can be permanent because energy changes and shifts constantly. All matter in your space has an orchestrated placement for a good reason. No accidents happen in your world's small arena. The stage is carefully prepared and planned. There are those in the spirit world who have devoted their lives to managing the world you live in. Do not cling to any object. Do not be attached to that which will never remain over a long period of time.

Many people are already aware of this.

SG-Once one achieves the ability to be detached from things other non-physical skills become easier.

Q- Does this mean that the gifts of spirit including clairvoyance, clairsentience, and clairaudience can only be achieved once one frees himself from dependence on physical matter?

Note-Saint Germain expressed the following paragraph very strongly. It was channeled on Christmas Eve, 2013 and answers the question above.

SG-Yes, very true. This is the message at a time of year when drama occurs around material things. Drama to have and possess more objects of dense energy. Perspective is missing and the emphasis is on obtaining more things—beyond personal necessity. We should be completely aware of the limited life of objects. It is fine to enjoy these objects, but the gifts of spirit, on the other hand, are more lasting. Your soul and the love you have for other souls can never disappear or be lost. Only this non—material energy is eternal.

Note-I commented that I love the way he expressed that and I wondered how we would incorporate this information in this work book? I did not have to wait long for an exercise to be suggested!

Exercise 1

SG- List 20 physical objects you believe that you love and could not live without. Secondly, list 20 non-physical things that have some connection with the 20 objects you've listed above. Choose a non-material word that is paired up with the physical object. This lesson is one of understanding what is real and unreal or seen and unseen. I immediately came up with the word money and paired it with service. I paired book with knowledge, and ring with love. See how many combinations you can find.

Exercise 2

List 10 things you have done this week to connect with other people. Write this on paper and carry it with you. This adds to the power of the service you have provided. When you acknowledge the connection with your brother it is a powerful affirmation and resonates in the spiritual realms.

Living in the world

Groups and Mobs

Q-As I channeled one morning suddenly I had a vision of a flock of seagulls. Is there some significance to this vision?

SG-Yes, the seagulls are a metaphor for the manner in which souls move in formation. This group movement is not a positive energetic choice as it clouds the soul's ability to see his or her own path. We shall talk about the mob.

Note- I made a couple of comments about the world in general and expressed my opinion that the planet earth is going in the wrong direction.

SG-We see this here in the spiritual realm. It is part of your planet's growth and why the physical world is not an easy place to be embodied. It is, however, a place that propels many souls forward rapidly if one stands apart from the mob.

Q-I don't understand what you mean by using the word mob. Can you explain this?

SG-The mob shares one mind and this is often begun by one individual with a powerful agenda. The leader with an agenda has an ability to incite the mob. He will take over the mind and the personal choice of others. A group is quite different. The group comes together to do good things in the world. Each has an individual mind and they work together. We encourage groups.

Q-Where is evidence of the mob happening now?

SG-It is with great sadness to say that in many places.

Q- I asked if he had any other comments about this world and how difficult it is sometimes it is to live in this period of history. He began to use the word saturation in the conversation. I was at first perplexed but as the conversation continued I began to understand the point he was making.

Saturation

sat·u·ra·tion:

The state or process that occurs when no more of something can be absorbed, combined with, or added.

When Saint Germain began talking about the word saturation I was a little confused. Then I realized what he was saying. The world we live in is completely over- saturated in physical matter. In other words, we have so many distractions in this material world that nothing more can be added. St. Germain says that we have to look very carefully at this and reevaluate the parts of our material life that do not serve us anymore. He wants us to eliminate those things that are unnecessary.

This is how he expresses this word:

SG-Saturation is the word we use to describe the density of materialism in the world of physicality. This space, in which you reside, is saturated – densely seeded with energy of what you may call self – need, self – righteousness, and personal entitlement. Some souls will come to you carrying this energy of need, and self-love to the extent that they are unable to reach out and understand their brother. So this dense energy must be broken and placed in the light of spiritual understanding. Think of this like an egg. The shell has hardened and its contents must be revealed. We are feathering the nest with debris – bits and pieces of pretty things but

22

nothing of importance. Dense physical matter which serves no higher purpose. This can be understood when you visit a store filled with noise, images, and distractions, to entice you to have more of nothing of any real importance. The most precious possessions do not have form. Prioritize and see the difference between those things that you need and those that are wasteful and unnecessary.

SG-Tell me what has meaning and what does not?

Jane- I answered him that the things that have meaning to me would be love, family, animals, good health, giving to others, being quiet, holding hands – things like that.

SG-Things are necessary but should only be perceived as the props to make everything else happen. When the props become more important than love for another soul a disconnection occurs at the source.

Q -When do people disconnect?

SG- When they forget the true meaning of why they are here. They are not here to buy a special car – not to own and accumulate things, but to serve others. There are many props with no substance.

He asked me to look around my home and make a list of all things of the soul. He then asked me to write a second list of all things not of the soul. He said, do you not see that one list is very short?

Jane-I agreed and commented that nothing in my room here is important except the conversation that I'm having with you. This conversation is valuable.

SG-Yes, so the short list is invisible?

Q-Do I understand correctly that the real world, which is invisible, is disconnected from the visible material world we live in?

SG- Yes I am pleased you understand the most important lesson. Place your focus on all thoughts of light and invisibility. Place no importance on the solid items you see as they do not have everlasting life. Love has everlasting life. Love lasts forever. The kitchen table or expensive dress is of little importance to your soul. Needs are to be expected. However, where a need become saturated it takes on the quality of deep longing and the feelings and energy of the owner become reversed. Need is acceptable, but love for an object which is saturated is not acceptable.

I loved the metaphor. What we should love is invisible. It's an interesting way of describing what is important and what is not.

Exercise:

SG-List your needs and state them clearly

I made my list which included car, house, paint brush, love, and quiet to hear spirit, prayer, peace, and forgiveness.

SG-This is a powerful lesson for your world which moves faster and faster into saturation and away from the light. He continued to say that despite the fact that many individuals understand this lesson already; the world is still moving in the direction of saturation and will continue that way for many centuries.

Q- This is very discouraging?

SG-There will be many who will begin to re-organize their thoughts. Each soul who realizes the difference between physicality and spirituality, the importance of spirit and the unimportance of material form will grow in spirit.

A Planetary Shift

This information was channeled in late December, 2013. Saint Germain uses the word revolution in describing a shift in our Planet's vibration and how it will affect those in the physical body.

Q- I was unaware a shift was forthcoming. Is the sun or any other planet involved in this shift?

SG-This shift is unrelated to other planetary bodies. The energy is created by embodied souls. Bodies of a higher vibration multiply and add fuel to the small flame. Many are feeling this now including yourself.

He asks me if my ability to hear spirit is getting louder and I answered yes.

SG-The energy rotates in a circular pattern around the earth. It creates motion and a pulsating energy that affects humans and animals. The energy is uncomfortable for many souls. Because of this they leave and return to spirit. Others, like you, will help the remaining ones attune to the energy.

Q-I commented that this sounds not only like a big responsibility, but a catastrophe like a weather event?

SG-Weather changes are affected by this energy. Storms and unexpected weather events will occur all over the planet. The timing occurs within the next 5 years. The old ways will fail and a new earth will be born.

He is referring here to all systems—government, religion, food supply, interpersonal relationships, housing and families. He tells me that I will be spending all my time as a messenger between spirit and earth. This was why I was born, to be here in this role at this time in history. The early signs are here. There is planetary warming, increasing numbers of spiritual seekers, higher rates of suicide and death, and more reliance on the powers of government and not the community of people gathered to help each other.

Q-This seems like a very hard time for people. Will we still have the use of all the technological devices like cars and computers?

SG-These will continue to serve as other devices are invented. Many souls will wake up spiritually during this time. Many, he says, will believe the earth changes are a signal that the anti-Christ is coming. This is not so. It is a time of re-birth and action to return to one's true nature.

Prayer for America:

And now we pray for America – the country deeply blessed to support all other nations in setting an example of freedom and personal autonomy for souls of the planet. Pray for the understanding that each soul has an individual purpose towards this goal of freedom, security, and love of the father above all else in their sojourn on the planet. Pray, that one may see and acknowledge this freedom. Power and strength is sent to all who love their country, its people, and walk the path of light and not capitulate into the dysfunctional material minded mob.

I answered that I did understand. It reminded me of the early settlers.

SG-Artificial cycles aren't healthy and create your society's preoccupation with stress. Practice a change in the perception of time. Like a settler on your planet managing their work without the little timepiece.

Q-I would like that but what is the benefit?

SG-To feel the energy of the planet in your world – to become one with it – to live like the small animals and plants, and nature spirits.

This places you in harmony with all that there is and raises your vibration significantly.

I told him that I would try to do this and he seemed pleased.

CHAPTER 4
FAMILY

Gracious father, I pray to be shown the greatest understanding and love for those souls of my choosing. My soul will soar to new heights as I overcome all obstacles to love. I challenge myself to bring love into every encounter. I challenge myself to be the peacemaker.

Q-Please talk about the family structure. What brings families together and what tears them apart? How is the decision made to be reincarnated together?

SG-This is a wonderful topic and know that families are made, not born. The family unit is the greatest teaching classroom for your soul. In this arrangement of persons who spend many years together, there can be many conflicts. Such disturbances are part of the soul's great challenge to love. There is careful planning and much discussion which is choreographed by spirit and Masters on the other side.

Q-How does this happen?

I am shown water which is forming whirlpools that spin into circles.

SG-Water forms whirlpools of energy. A circle of souls begins to pull together in formation. There is energy or force pulsating and pulling them together.

Q-What if souls are at different levels of soul growth? Do they still hold together?

SG-Souls at all levels find and are drawn toward others. It is as natural as the ocean forming beautiful waves – like the waves and the action of waves. When a particular family unit forms here from where I speak to you, master teachers, angels, and even I may intercede in the discussions.

Q- There are so many souls and this sounds like so much work?

SG-This work is accomplished with care. The spirit world is well served by souls who are here specifically to monitor and supervise this process.

Q-Is this all about choice? Some souls come into a family and then commit suicide. Can you comment on suicide?

SG-Taking one's life is a concern for all parties joining the family group. This is often discussed by the family. It is not an easy process. This action is a serious learning experience for many. The soul that volunteers to leave may do so to assist other souls in their growth, or simply to reject the physical world all together.

Q-So it is a decision to help others or simply exit prematurely?

SG-Yes, correct and always a serious decision managed by guides.

Q-Some people come to me for help because they have experienced difficult relationships with their parents, particularly their mothers. Is this planned?

SG- Souls do unto others as others do unto them. A balancing of the energy is necessary, and each soul will choose a lifetime to experience and participate in this. Whether an individual soul rises to the challenge in the physical body is another issue. All parties leave here with the challenge, very few complete the task at 100%. You might say that some get a B+. So success varies.

Q- Help me with some information for my readers as they approach Thanksgiving. How do the readers manage this holiday with their families, especially if there's negative energy or bad feelings between them?

SG-Take a moment to quietly remember that you have all been asked to board this ship together. All have a job to do in making it to the ships final destination. The quarters are very tight so anger, resentment, and territorial issues can set a negative tone. All sailors must pitch in and care for each other as they journey across the wide ocean. Each has a role on the ship. Each has a challenge – Some more than others. Perhaps, a sailor is ill or deformed and needs the crew to care for him? Perhaps, a sailor falls off one boat into the water. The others will try to rescue him or her and may or may not be successful. All hands on deck!

Q-So this is a reminder that there are no accidents? When a family gathers for Thanksgiving or other holidays they are with the souls of their choice. Is it is also true for those individuals coming into the family due to marriage?

SG-Some individuals have multiple families and this is also accepted as the souls challenge.

Q-What about mothers who abandon their children?

SG-Such an occurrence has many reasons behind it.

Q- I wondered if this could have something to do with karma.

SG-The word karma is misleading. This is too simple for the process. The task is more complicated and sophisticated. Like a spider with a delicate web not all threads are perfect.

Note- Karma is associated with re-birth or reincarnation. One's actions in the present life can affect those in the future.

Q-Please give us some special guidelines to help families get through the holidays together.

SG-Holy Father we send light and everlasting understanding to the families gathering together in groups this holiday. We pray that they are conscious of the law of love. Love others as you would like to be loved yourself. Forgive others as you would ask to be forgiven. Be in remembrance of the divine love given to each soul in this moment. This family was born in spirit. Amen.

Q- Is there something they could do during the day if there were difficulties?

SG- When conflict takes place, and no resolution has been given, one may say, I choose this individual to be in my life. I release all the pain and suffering they have caused me. I do not expect the same from them as they may not be ready to forgive me. I love all souls gathered around the table today. I choose to live my life with their support.

Marital relationships

SG-All beings seek love. Every soul is love and the union of two souls is sought after with great vigor. Sometimes this union is perfectly balanced, calm, and in perfect time. There are relationships which begin before the appointed moment and create a change in the souls plan for this partnership.

Q-Is this because we choose relationships before we come into the body?

SG-Yes, that is correct. There is a plan as we have discussed previously, and not all plans proceed in a timely fashion. Once the union of souls comes together as planned in the spiritual realms, each soul is given additional assistance to bring it to its completion. Just as you begin writing a book you must complete it. There are spirits who help you in this endeavor, and so it is the same with partnerships of love, or partnerships of hate.

Q-How do you know you have the right partner? The person you chose before birth?

SG-This is a great question. The one who has chosen will appear in your life one day and there will be a signal. This is so both of you will remember the agreement.

Q-What kind of signal should people look for?

SG-The signal is a feeling, vision, or words. There is always a message. There is an attempt by angelic guidance to establish a strong signal and bring it into focus. Everyone who has entered into a partnership of love, hate, or indifference can recall the signal if they choose to do so. Once the signal is recognized, energy is sent to the couple in order to move the relationship forward. This assistance is powerful and very few souls can bypass it. Those who believe they should have never met a particular person are incorrect. Relationship is not always easy. Just because something is difficult does not eliminate the prior appointment. Partnerships are carefully worked out and there is a reason for each one.

Q-How can we help people prepare for these partnerships?

SG-We must first establish that all relationships in which there are strong feelings, images, or unusual thoughts are likely to be relationships with the purpose of continuing one's soul's growth. Once the signal has been felt, seen, or heard, we provide a meditation to take this to the next step.

Please see the meditation at the end of this chapter.

Q- Please comment on levels of energy. I understand that everything is energy but sometimes we have to interact with people at different levels of energy. What if two people in relationship are operating at a different level of energy? For instance, someone has a very low frequency and her partner has a very high level of energy and they are in a close relationship or married. How does this work?

SG-When a highly evolved soul is associated with one that is not there can be a disruption in the relationship. The relationship cannot continue unless there was a strong reason for beginning it originally. So this is the question one may ask – why am I here with this energy? What can I do to raise it up? Can I work with it? Is it my special pledge to work with this person?

Q-Let's say someone has permission to work with this person. What do they do to help themselves and the other person?

SG- They must practice patience and kindness. Love this person knowing they are God. The task at hand is one of great sensitivity. When one enters a relationship with a person who has a slower vibration the challenge is to lift them up. This challenge, when successfully handled, has positive implications for the growth of the soul.

Q- Was this a contract made before coming into the body?

SG- Yes, in some instances. In other situations it may not have been previously planned and there may be a separation coming up at a future time. Those who have pledged to work together will have support from us here in maintaining the relationship.

Exercise: Relationship Meditation

It is not necessary to have an actual partner for this meditation. The purpose of this exercise is to help one determine the strength of a relationship.

Sit quietly and imagine this other person sitting in a chair before you. Reach out, take their hands, and look into their eyes. Say, I am seeing you before me and believe you were meant to enter my life. We have made an agreement to work together in this life. Please tell me if you believe this is true as well?

Stay quiet and be patient. Wait for your partner to answer. This person will speak to you in the meditation. Listen to the answer and write down the first thing you hear, feel, and sense. Trust this information and thank your partner.

Graciously acknowledge your partners response. Declare in one sentence the essence of your work together. Ask your partner to agree or disagree and write it down.

Ask your partner to list all the life tasks you will perform together. Write these down. Secondly, record all the life tasks you see for this partnership. Thank the person and send them love.

Take this information which is the list of the work you will accomplish together and expand on the words in order to create sentences. Create a mission statement. I (your name) pledge to fulfill my soul agreement to the best of my ability. I bless my partner and know that together we will experience great spiritual growth and understanding.

Q-What if somebody does not understand or get the signal?

SG- If there is no signal it is a false start. Do not be hasty to enter into a holy agreement. All relationships are holy and the bad relationships are often the most holy and life- altering partnerships.

Q-What about male – female. Does it matter?

SG-No, gender is not an issue. One takes on the physical vehicle of all genders, and although one may prefer female over male, they all have something to teach. You may try this exercise yourself and be surprised. Now we pray.

Prayer for Relationships:

Blessings to all who enter into relationships with higher understanding. Such associations are a learning experience for each soul. This is the best use of your time on earth. No other relationship is as powerful as that between the two who have made an agreement to learn together in the body. All other associations, although learning experiences, are weak in comparison. Know and recognize the signs. One is encouraged to understand the messages. Help is always offered.

CHAPTER 5
BODY, SOUL
MIND

Body is only the vehicle. The soul is the rider. The soul is light and emanates from the center of the heart chakra. One's soul is precious. The soul is life and without it the body dies and so we will discuss the care of the soul.-Saint Germain.

Q-How is a soul born?

SG-This is a complicated issue and it is difficult from a human standpoint to grasp the intricacies of the process. Souls are created by God. Just as souls are born, they also require the need to live again in physical form. This is a continuous cycle.

The energy of the soul emerges outward into a circular formation. It is implanted with some knowledge before birth into a body. It is like an infant. They remain in spirit for a period of time to be nurtured. They are assisted in choosing their first physical vehicle. The first incarnation represents an important marker for the soul and imprints it in special ways.

Note- In my case, I spent the first few incarnations on a planet where my body was only 25% physical matter and the rest energy. When I was born into a physical body here on earth I was told the density of the body had both strengths and limitations for me. I was able to relate to this information.

Q- Is there a specific place where a soul is born?

SG- No, this is not a place but a vibration.

SG-The soul is empowered by love, and as I send love the light grows. The more love it receives the wider the expansion of the light. This expansion transcends its location in the heart chakra and goes beyond the body. This light, which is powerful energy, moves outward. It touches everything in its space. Soul energy expands and grows. Those whose soul light has been dimmed can be helped simply by the extension of another soul's light.

Note-I found this very interesting because we can empower and assist other souls by simply helping them to expand their soul energy.

SG- I will teach you a technique for soul expansion.

A lesson in expanding love

SG-Imagine a round pebble. It is dark and small. Let light shine upon it and watch the pebble expanding and changing color. Take a moment to do this.

Jane- I was able to see a pink and white light with a halo extending beyond the pebble

SG-Now send it love and light. Do this now.

Jane- I could see this pebble pulsating, getting larger.

SG-Watch the outer edges.

I did this and saw bands of light emanating out from the ball.

SG-Move the bands of light outward. Make it happen.

I found myself pulling them out and small balls began to form at the ends.

SG- Gently throw these balls outward to share the love. Remember, he said, this is like plucking grapes.

Note- Saint Germain instructed me to practice this with everybody. He said to observe the light in the heart chakra. As you see this light it will tell you how much love the person needs.

Q-Could you clarify this for me?

SG- A heart with no light lacks love. The larger the circle of light, the greater the souls love for himself and the greater their ability to share this love with others.

Note- In other words we must love ourselves before we can give it to others.

Q- How can I expand someone's love if there is none to hold on to?

He was very excited when I asked this question.

SG- You may send some of your light to them first. The first step is to look and see. Evaluate – if necessary, share your light by sending it directly to the heart. Then you begin to expand the light that exists in their soul. This is powerful love energy. The more souls who practice sharing this love in the world, the better the energy of the planet.

I commented that it sounds very simple but what if someone is unable to see the light?

SG- It is not that simple. Only those with expanded souls of love can do this. As you give you will receive.

Holy Father of the most immense universe, we pray that many souls with dark burdens of pain and sorrow will be lifted up to the power in energy of love. This is all we have – love – and its opposite, fear and sorrow. We pray that the love will be expressed despite strong opposition.

Physical Body

Your body is like the vehicle you drive. You control it. You—the real you—fit inside and decide to travel north, south, east, or west. The vehicle might begin to fall apart. Some will not repair it; others will keep it in good shape. Spiritual growth happens when the vehicle is well-cared for. This allows the higher vibrations and information in. - Saint Germain

SG- When you are born into a body, both the body and the soul are energy. The combination of the two creates the energy signature of the person. Maintaining a healthy body assures the soul's ability to do its work and to fulfill its mission on the planet. Poor body care will bring the focus away from the soul and point to physical dis—ease. This is why the topic is so important. To surrender to the body and its dis-ease is the common manner in which your fellow humans operate. The body is nothing. The body is controlled by the soul. The soul is master. Take charge of this gift. Like any object you buy, own, or are gifted with, maintenance is important. Healing is an individual responsibility. At birth each of us brings a small book containing a list of ailments that we agree to battle in the life ahead. Some carry a small book and others agreed to manage a heavier load.

Q- What does my book look like?

SG-You brought in a moderately heavy book, with emphasis on the bones.

Q- Can you comment on my neck, which has given me some problems?

SG- The neck is a pivotal point. All the worry, doubt, fear and anxiety rush upwards to this area of the body. Imagine a pole that is battered by storms. It begins to sway and shift. That is your neck.

He then continued to give me a prayer to heal my neck.

SG- Please say, "I am the divine aspect of the Father, and I heal my structure. I replace the old house with a new one." One must be fully in charge of the physical vehicle. To leave the vehicle alone is to invite illness. One must never neglect that which is a support.

Q- How can one heal prior damage without surgery or handle many years in which the body has been neglected?

SG-The body house is replaced thousands of times in a lifetime. One can always re-visit and take control unless the vehicle has been neglected too long. Some souls make the decision to leave and do so by neglecting the body.

Note-This is one of the most important points in the book. If you are having physical difficulties, there is a spiritual solution. Ask in the name of the Holy Father this physical problem you are dealing with be replaced with something better. The body is sacred as it provides a vehicle for the soul.

SG -You live in spirit, not body. Body is only a temporary condition – an abstraction. Spirit is real. We love you and all spirits of the universe. We are here to help you into the knowledge of who you really are.

Q- I asked him to comment on the possibility that a spiritual problem could actually cause a physical illness. I had read a book which lists the physical ailment and its spiritual cause?

SG- It is true as there is a binding connection between mind, soul, and body so no one can escape this fact. Determining the spiritual or metaphysical cause and matching it to the physical disease is not an easy task and cannot be published in a book. When faced with this question, I will assist you in making the diagnosis.

Q-I asked St. Germain to explain to me the situation that exists when somebody is in a coma. While I was writing this book the former Israeli Prime Minister, Ariel Sharon, died after spending eight years in a coma. Does a soul choose this? Does the soul leave the body, or do they stay within the body? Is it something chosen by a soul before they even come into a physical body, or is it an accident?

SG-One may choose this manner of leaving the physical dimension, or it may choose him. Each situation is different. When one becomes comatose, they can remain hidden in the physical form, or immediately come to the light. This decision is the souls right. Guides here become involved, but cannot make this decision for the comatose individual. In the case of Sharon, he remained in body as a symbol to the people of Israel, but his soul was here. Only small soul parts remained with the body as a necessity to maintain the life force for such a long time. And so, the answer is not one answer but has variables.

Food

Q-Could you speak about the diet we eat on planet earth?

SG- Maintaining a healthy body assures the soul's ability to work and fulfil his or her mission on earth.

SG-The land yields poorer substances for the body as compared to previous centuries. This makes food choices more difficult. The body was not intended as a vessel for animal meats. The body is a vessel for anything coming from the earth – anything planted in the earth.

He tells us to keep food simple. Vegetables, fruit, little meat and no fish.

Q-Why eliminate fish?

SG- Only three places exist on earth where it is safe to eat fish and of a fresh catch.

Q- Where are these places?

SG- Northern Russia, Norway and Iceland.

Q-I mentioned that I was a vegetarian and asked if I should give up my eggs?

SG- Eggs from clean chickens are good.

Q- What about meat? Most people say they require this?

SG- They are convinced by all the emotional messages from those who would convince them it is a healthy practice. These messages are not in the interest of anyone. Meat is almost always rotten before cooking. Once eaten, meat rots in the body creating toxins. This does not lighten or purify it. When an animal is caught and slaughtered right away, and eaten quickly, as done in primitive societies, this was better for the people.

Q-What about drinking alcohol particularly wine- my personal favorite?

SG-This is the planet of artificial and mind/body altering substances. I think it is a wonder that anyone can think in this century.

I agreed with him that drugs are abused.

SG- No pills! Eliminate all unnecessary foreign substances in the body. Alcohol in large amounts should be eliminated. Wine is a substance when used in moderate amounts is helpful to the body and has been drunk since man discovered a taste of the grape.

I was happy to hear this about the wine.

SG-The body is not the master. The soul is the master. When body troubles come, take charge. Say to the body "I am not a body, I am part of the divine power of God, and in this capacity I demand the body to heal. I demand to give this body's pain or restriction over to the Holy Father." The body is here to allow the fulfillment of your soul's agreement in this life. The body will misbehave if the soul is not in alignment with its purpose. Always ask yourself, what

42

is my body trying to teach me, and then take your right of God-centered power to insist on healing.

Q-Most people do not believe they have a choice when facing a physical illness?

SG- The soul is always chief. Body/mind loves to bring discord. Remember, you are a Holy Spirit. You are light. Strong auras exist around those who are aware of them. They add strength to protect the body.

Q- So the body is sacred?

SG-Yes, but only insofar as it provides a vehicle for the soul.

Q- So what do we need to do?

SG-Refuse to be a member of the mob. Eat plants. Fill your body with the light from the sun.

Pray "Holy Father, I request your assistance in bringing light into my body so that my mission embodied may be accomplished more successfully."

SG-Use drugs only when no other natural alternative exists. Good food is the best medicine. Throw away drugs and cigarettes. Cigarettes will stop the soul from progressing as they will place a black cloud over the aura. Walk every day in nature. Fancy exercise is not important. Take time for quiet and reflection. Start now.

Q-What about controlling anxiety?

SG- This will come as the soul's path is fully understood. Pray, "Holy Father, please guide me to the light of my soul – to the task I have agreed to accomplish while in this physical vehicle. Body is only the vehicle. The soul is the rider."

Energy Body

SG-Just as the physical body must be cared for and maintained, so must the energy matrix which surrounds you. The energy body is bombarded daily with the emotions, hurts, good feelings, worries, and anxiety of others.

I told St. Germain that I already knew some techniques to cloak my energy.

SG-This is not nearly enough. There is a need for a retraction of the body. Just as you pick up a cold, you may bring home a worry or an emotional hurt plucked off the person sitting in the area beside you.

Q- Is this the aura?

SG It is, and I offer a technique for those that may have sensitive energy bodies.

Shrinking the energy body

SG-Imagine yourself taking a shower before going out. Feel your energy shrink. While you are out hold the dampness and wetness close to you and keep it sprayed. Your energy will increase and your mood will be lighter when not caring the burdens of others on top of your own.

I mentioned that this sounded like a cosmic holy shower. He loved the analogy.

Soul Colors

SG-A soul color is not the soul's aura. It is deeper than that, and always remains the same at the time of the person's incarnation. Color is a vibration also. I will assist you in identifying the color as you continue to work with people. Colors are significant and are always a mixture. Red is the color of power and may get souls in trouble. The mis-use of red is seen in the world today. A red soul may, however, be called to a higher level of action.

Q-What about Hitler' soul color?

SG- He was a red soul without the supporting colors. Soul colors are almost always a mixture. You are a blue soul with tints of yellow and violet.

SG- Blue is the harmony of love-a color associated with those on a high spiritual path. The violet is your connection to us, and yellow is your love of learning.

Q- I asked about my husband Don?

SG- He is a green soul and therefore loves the earth. His presence brings healing to others. Tints of red bring power and he carries this energy in the correct amount. Blue is the color that helps him connect to spirit.

Q- Can colors change?

SG- Yes, they change throughout one's life.

Q- What about white?

SG- White is the absence of color but almost always includes other bits of color as well. New souls are clothed in white and as they gain life experience they also gain color.

Mind and Thoughts

Please stop hurting yourself with thoughts. Your thoughts are more powerful than you are able to imagine right now. Think only of that which you desire. Be that which you desire. - Saint Germain

These were the first words spoken to me by St. Germain. He said them with great strength and power. It is a lesson for all of us that our thoughts create our reality.

Q- You say thoughts are powerful, but do they have substance?

SG- This is a complicated issue. Yes, thoughts are things and they do form an energetic signature. In this way they do have a type of form, but not like a physical form. As you know, one is able to feel the energy of a person. The energy of both body and mind are joined.

Q- I have heard that sound can take away thoughts?

SG- Sound is powerful and you hear the higher vibrations yourself, do you not? Sounds which cause great distress to animals will destroy thoughts at the energetic level.

Q- Would this high pitched sound destroy negative dark energy also?

SG- Yes, it will cause any negative thought or uncomfortable energy emerging from the mind to be destroyed immediately.

Q- Why do so few people know this?

SG- It is a healing modality and must be used with care by those who understand it. Over use can cause harm to animals, plants, and humans who spend too much time in the vibration. It must also be used in a closed space.

He went on to tell me that just as sound is powerful, so is light energy.

Q- Can we send thoughts to others?

SG- Thoughts are things—energy messages. Think of a thought like a post card sent immediately to a recipient. Take care with your message as it will affect the receiver. This is why thoughts are so important. Send thoughts of love all the time. Practice this and the energy will be multiplied and sent back to you.

SG-The mind must always be where we are at the soul level despite the activity of the body. Trust that heavenly beings working with you will be pushing you forward and faster if you become more focused. You are a magician and can create anything you desire. Stand firm and tall and tell the universal energy that you accept all gifts it has prepared for you. Watch your thoughts. Any negative thought will impact another soul. Send love not hate. Write down each person you send love to today. Do one kind thing for someone. This can be simple—carry bags or say hello. Live outside of yourself, not inside. Be open. Do not hide within the safe barriers built by many. This helps to manage the dark places.

Q- Could you explain what is meant by the dark places?

SG-One may become obsessed with earthly pursuits and some of these are dark and obstruct the true nature of a spiritual being. Books and movies may take one to these dark places. Obsession with the body and desire for mind-altering experiences is not safe for soul or body and lead one to the dark places. Focus on love, kindness and compassion instead of violence, substance abuse, and violent language. Do you understand?

I answered yes, that this made complete sense to

CHAPTER 6

ANGELS, GUIDES, ORBS, GOD

Blessed Father who brings the love of connection between spirits in and out of the body, Angels, and guardians, we bless those souls who willingly seek to establish a powerful spiritual bond, which is necessary for overcoming the obstacles of the physical world. Reading this book and agreeing to participate in the message is a sign to your guides and Angels that you are ready to take the next step in your spiritual growth. This step will save you from repeating the lessons of both the current or previous lifetimes. Bless you, and know that you are never alone for any minute of any day, and so my dear child, stand within the light you may not see, but which protects and loves you always. Amen.

Q-What proof is there that spirit exists?

SG-Spirit is everywhere. Take a moment and think about your life and all the times spirit intervened on your behalf. Spirit often intervenes when it is not time to leave the body. Some of you have experienced a close call such as an accident or illness which leaves you wondering how you survived. When this happens spirit has crossed your path. Some are very lucky to hear and see spirit, and others have not taken the time to develop this ability.

Q-What is the difference between an angel and a guide?

SG- A guide is a being who chooses to stand by your side through-out your physical life-time. One may have one or more guides. Relatives who have passed into spirit often volunteer to take on this responsibility. This is a major decision. To guide a soul is a major responsibility. It is a "self-less" task and the guide must postpone their own work. Old souls are, therefore the best candidates for this work. A guide never leaves your side even when you sleep. An angel has always existed in the spiritual realms and has never been embodied.

Angels have souls but not of the same essence as those who evolve in physical bodies. Angels are created by the universal love you call the Holy Father or all there is.

Q- How are guides and angels paired up with particular people?

SG- This is a very involved process which is partially accomplished in the spiritual realm. Guides are chosen based on spiritual knowledge and past involvement with the soul. Angels are also assigned to each person based on this person's level of spiritual understanding and knowledge. It is, however, a mutual decision. All you need to know is that angels and guides are carefully matched to you. The physical plane is very distracting and spirit connection can be very difficult in the density of the physical world. Guides create change and provide instruction despite the lack of a seemingly visible connection.

Q- Can a guide intervene and change something in our lives?

SG- Yes, a guide may intervene in situations where one's life path is detouring from the original blue-print. The guide must confer with one's council here in spirit before intervening.

Q-When I conduct a reading for a client I am often given the opportunity to speak with one or more members of their council. Can you tell me more about this?

SG- This is a group of elder souls who work with you between lives. They oversee everything that is happening in your current life. They always have your highest good at the forefront of any decision.

Q- I am often asked, how do I connect with my own angels and guides?

SG- Communicating with spirit is an ability all have. Are you not a spirit inhabiting a human body? It is important to make the time for this relationship. It is a relationship like any other. You and your guides are a TEAM. Once you acknowledge that this relationship is important, spirit will speak loudly.

He continues to say that our guides are anxious to speak with us. They are present and waiting for us to reach out to them. Although we may feel alone, the earth is densely seeded with ancient wisdom and love.

SG-As you walk through your daily tasks, spirit walks with you. Pray for guidance. Ask to see the divine in the greater world of form. As you go through your day look upward instead of down. Ask for guidance from the heavens.

St. Germain summoned the Archangel Raphael to talk more about the angelic realm.

Archangel Raphael - I speak first to convey the message from the brigade of angelic hosts who provide support to all living bodies on the planet. We desire recognition and much to our dismay, this is lacking in over 70% of the world's people. In your world it is easy to deny the presence of the Angels. We exist and work diligently to make ourselves known. I give you instructions to help you with making a connection with us"

Connecting with your Angels

Meditation

Archangel Raphael-Choose a quiet place to do this meditation. Make sure you have a journal in which to record the information.

Imagine a phone box like the ones of the past when someone places a coin in the slot and makes a phone call. Enter this box and close the door. You have stepped into a safe place. Outside of the box there is a garden. Nobody walks there and there are no noises to distract you. Pick up the telephone and dial "my angel."

The phone will ring a few times and a voice will answer. The voice will say who is calling? Respond to the voice with your birth date and request to have a conversation with your angel.

When I entered the box which was covered with gold. I saw a white phone and I dialed the number.

When the voice answers with the name of your guardian angel she will say, "I am pleased to speak with you. Do you have a question for me?"

Archangel Raphael - You may ask as many questions as you would like and agree to a second meeting or call. You determine the place and your angel will meet you.

I expressed my concern to the Archangel Raphael that my readers might have difficulty seeing, feeling or hearing words.

Archangel Raphael - The first experience will be Clairsentience. Feel the air, vibrations, and the environment. The angel will try to give you a sign. Be aware and alert. Write down the sign and your feelings. This is a simple visual exercise to open up doors

I thanked Archangel Raphael and then St. Germain returned.

SG- This is a first step in helping individuals understand that they are not a soloist jumping out of an airplane. They are covered. The pilot is an angel, and the angels are softening the fall. There is no such thing as the word alone. We put a large letter X on this terrible word. You are never alone.

Written exercise to "power-up" your connection with your angels and guides

Complete the following sentences:

I, _____ feel my guardian angel. I feel them every_____.

I, _____ can sense my guide behind me. I feel his presence most frequently during _____.

I, _____ pledge to make the acquaintance with my guide in this physical world and request their help.

I,_____ will pledge to spend 15 minutes each day, either upon waking or going to sleep, to reach out to my angels and guides. In turn, they pledge to respond to me.

I, _____ am most comfortable seeing, hearing, feeling, or communicating in writing with my guides. Select one.

At least twice a day seek guidance in order to make this relationship happen. Do not expect the connection to happen immediately. With effort you will be successful.

SG- In this exercise you practice reaching upward to connect with spirit. Angels and guides will not hesitate to meet you in between. This exercise is powerful and with a fearless intention will yield results. Write down your feelings and thoughts when they appear to come quickly and spontaneously, for these are words of wisdom and guidance. Like any relationship, this one takes time and practice. Friendships are not created instantly, and the same is true in connecting with your guides and angels. A strong bond of trust and love must be established.

A Prayer for the Angels

Blessed are those beautiful lights on earth. All lights come together and become brighter. Angelic forces are wound like threads around groups of souls and the light expands. Know that all gatherings of souls and angels send blinding light outward to affect the planet earth. We pray that this awareness becomes known to all. Love and light is sent from the heavenly plains – not alone, but on earth. Amen. Saint Germain

Orbs

Q-I have always been very curious about orbs. These are round objects often caught on film. I have photographed quite a few, particularly in sacred places like Ireland. What are these?

SG-These phenomena as some refer to it, are now emerging into the light as more of you raise your consciousness and begin to see and feel the presence of these beings. As you know, all of you are surrounded and protected by angelic beings who offer support to you before birth. These orbs also offer assistance to you. They are spiritual beings, not from another dimension, and available to you for your protection and enlightenment. You may call on them and ask that they show themselves to you at any time.

Q- Can you explain in more detail the service the orbs provide?

Q- They are called "the watchers." The emotional energy of the physical world is softened by their presence. You might think of them as spirits who clean things up as they keep the air fresh and clear of negativity. To see them is a blessing.

Q-I have noticed that the interior of these circles have distinctive patterns and colors. Can you tell me more about this?

SG-Each orb, like you, has a gift and a certain personality – not of the body but of the spirit. The inner beauty you see is a reflection of you as well as the beings themselves.

Q- Are they intelligent beings in their own right and a reflection of the humans they are attracted to?

SG- No, not necessarily. It is a mutual arrangement of respect and service.

God

Q – We are God because God is in us, but is God greater than us or are we all equal? What about gender—does God have a gender?

SG-This is an excellent question. God is all there is including the celestial bodies, the universe, the material and spiritual worlds. God is you. All parts of God are equal, but the source of this energy is greater than its parts. Do you understand?

Q- Yes, but how much bigger is the source?

SG-There is no size to be defined as the source is in constant motion sending energy outward to support the universe.

Q- Is this source male or female?

SG- There is no gender associated with that which is all powerful and holds and maintains the structure of such a vast and unlimited space.

Q- I mentioned that he always starts prayers with the Holy Father?

SG – Yes, with some humor. This is only to have a manner of speech which feels comfortable for you. We will now say Holy Father, Holy Mother, or Holy Source of all that exists.

CHAPTER 7
SPIRITUAL GIFTS

I found this to be some of the most interesting information I received from Saint Germain because of my own abilities to hear, see and sense spirits. I was told that those of us, who are aware of, and use, these gifts resonate at a high vibrational level and this energy can be uncomfortable if left un-engaged. It is also important to know that all gifts of spirit are messages. We all have these gifts, but like anything else in life we need to pay attention and cultivate them.

SG- There are many souls here on earth that carry the energy of spirit and do not allow it to expand and flourish. They must use the gifts to help those around them. The energy surrounds the body and bounces from one energy center to another. To control this vibration one must use it. Left by itself the energy is overwhelming and causes anxiety. Release the energy by putting it to good use.

Q- People who possess these gifts don't always feel that they fit in?

SG- There is no need to fit in.

Q- How does one develop these gifts?

SG- We begin with Clairsentience which is gaining knowledge through the senses. It is often the first gift and the one most easily recognized.

My first experience with this gift arrived through smell. I have always had a powerful nose. When I smell gardenias in a closed room I know my father, who loved this flower, is close by. My keen smell saved my family when a fire broke out in our garage on the other side of the house. I was just laying down for a nap and smelled smoke. I have also felt physical sensations, particularly when doing a reading for someone. Sometimes it is a feeling of pressure on my shoulder and back as if someone is resting their hand there; other times air seems to blow towards me while I sit in a closed room. I pay close attention and try to decipher the message. Sometimes it is simply an acknowledgement of what I am doing at that moment.

Q- What about Clairaudience or clear hearing?

SG-Hearing my voice is a more demanding skill requiring attention and acknowledgement of the connection. Hearing spiritual guidance is often dismissed as one's thoughts. There is a distinction between one's own thoughts and that of spirit. Love and compassion are contained in a spirit message. It is guidance on the highest level coming through the auditory canal.

Q- I know when spirit appears because of a buzzing or high pitched tone in my ears. Please describe clairvoyance or clear seeing?

SG- This is the last gift to be activated. It is connected to the crown chakra. Seeing is possible inside and outside the eye's function. You see when your eyes are closed—do you not?

 I answered yes to that question.

Q- Is it possible to be clairvoyant and not possess the other two gifts?

SG- Yes, this often happens when one is dominant and the other un-noticed.

Developing the Gifts

SG- At sunrise be aware of spirit. Before your mind takes control. Meditate in the first moment of the awake state. This calms the energy and affords the opportunity to ask for assistance for the day ahead.

Exercise to Develop Spiritual Gifts

Clairsentience-Clear Feeling

Identify at least 5 senses every day that appear to be messages. The message is delivered quickly and like an arrow toward the lower part of the body. Write down the sensations and next to each sensation interpret the message. If only one or two are perceived, that is all that is recorded. One must become a hunter of sensations – on the prowl for the communication. The sensations may involve taste, smell, feeling, or non-ordinary body feelings of hot and cold. - No soul lacks these messages.

Clairaudience – Clear Hearing

A tone or buzzing in the ears is often a sign of spirit's presence. Write down all the sounds that appear to be unusual. Write down all thoughts that appear to be outside of you. The thought occurs as if it was spoken by an outside party. Write down as many as you receive and the activity you were engaged in at the moment. Thirdly, record the message.

This is my strongest gift. The key to understanding it is to never dismiss a message that comes into your thoughts and feels as if someone is speaking to you. There is a difference between the chatter of the mind and a clear message from spirit and you can become very good at knowing the difference.

Clairvoyance- Clear seeing

This is a visual exercise. Close your eyes and see a place that you are familiar with in your current life. This should be a place where you feel safe and calm. No one will hurt or disturb you in this safe place. Look around and get your bearings. What is the weather like and how do you feel? Walk forward and pay attention to what you see on the ground, in the sky and the surrounding area. Pay attention if you see animals or other people. Remember what someone says to you. Open your eyes and return. Write down what you see and interpret the objects and symbols. Do this each day for 20 days. Always begin at the same place. This starting point will become familiar to you and the visual images will become stronger. Open eyes are the last to activate and only for those achieving the highest vibration of love.

A Prayer concerning the gifts of spirit:

Bless you who strive for a connection to the home of your soul. There is a vast dimension filled with love and support for those still in physical form. Reach out to us here and trust that we will respond. Your attention is required—nothing else. The gifts of the spirit are gifts for all and not held back from any soul. It is your task to develop these gifts and apply them to your life. All is love and connection, and you are love embodied.

CHAPTER 8
UNIVERSAL SYMBOLS

"Signs are placed everywhere by your angels and guides. They are sent in large quantities and must not be missed."- Saint Germain

When I asked Saint Germain to expound on exactly what signs we should be looking for he listed the following:

SG-Numbers, words spoken by others, books, colors, random thoughts, accidents, illness, body problems, music, animal behavior, seeing nature spirits, found objects—the list is endless. The upper realms of spirit are constantly guiding us and we are always directed to take a particular course of action.

Archangel Raphael- The signs are very personal and relate directly to you and your life's circumstances. We use whatever method will capture your attention and will activate the deeper areas of the brain to make you attentive to the message.

SG- We will start with one of the most common symbols in the physical world.

Time

The start of a new year is very artificial. Any day may represent the beginning of a new life, or a new goal. All time and the numbers representing it are insignificant. Time is an illusion—a smoke screen.

St. Germain began this discussion by pointing out my little timepiece which is an antique watch I keep on my desk.

SG- Too much time, too little time, out of time; time – challenged – so many frustrations related to this issue. You speak of time as if it was a real object or a person. Time ran out.

We both had good laugh!

SG- We will set the record straight. Time does not exist. Time is, like other material things, created by you. We do not live for time here in the spirit realms. We live moment to moment. Day and night do not constitute time as you define it. We may create day and night, but not time.

Note- Time is a man-made phenomenon to measure the movement of the earth around the sun. Nothing more.

Q-How can we can escape the fact of time? Everything here in this world is based on time?

SG- Good observation but we still throw it away. Use your little clock to fly away from time.

Saint Germain was referring to a little timepiece I bought with an eagle on the back side.

SG-Be time ignorant, time dead, time blind. Do you understand?

Q- I said no because I have to be on time for things. I asked him to help me.

SG-We begin with no time. On the clock there are no numbers. Discard the numbers and change numbers to read daylight, twilight, evening, and night. This is the energy of your planetary cycle, not a timepiece. We describe the day as morning, the early afternoon, and so forth. Do you see?

Note- When numbers are replaced by events (morning, evening, night) they cease to be repressive. They create less anxiety.

I answered that I did understand and it reminded me of the early settlers.

SG-Artificial cycles aren't healthy and create your society's preoccupation with stress. Practice a change in the perception of time. Pretend you are a settler on your planet managing your work without the little timepiece.

Q- I would like to do that but what is the benefit?

SG- To feel the energy of the planet in your world – to become one with it – to live like the small animals and plants and nature spirits. This places you in harmony with all that there is and raises your vibration significantly.

I told him that I would try to do this and he seemed pleased.

Numbers

Finding Your Birth Number: My birth date is June 12, 1951. June is the sixth month. I add all the numbers together $6 + 1 + 2 + 1 + 9 + 5 + 1 = 25$.   This double digit number should be broken down by adding $2 + 5 = 7$.   Seven is my birth number. If you add up all the digits and get a 10, you birth number is a 1.

SG- Numbers are significant and are part of the universal language. Their meaning goes back to the creation of the universe. Numbers are road signs.

The road signs are the messages that are sent to us every minute of every day. Everywhere we turn there is spiritual guidance if only we pay attention. Most days are a blur and we miss important information.

Q- Are birth numbers significant?

SG- Each soul chooses their number before birth. It represents the life forces and represents our connection to the celestial bodies. These symbols affect one's daily life in ways most people do not realize. To ignore or dismiss the number's message creates a tension that becomes uncomfortable and leaves one with a feeling that something is missing. The soul chooses the number and the essence of the life in physical body.

Q- Would you give me your interpretation of the meaning of one's life path number?

One is a powerful number and represents the connection of all souls in unity of love and purpose—both in and out of the body. The number resonates in the soul as a reminder of this connection. The number 10 breaks down in to a number one. A prayer for this number:

Holy Father, please help me to acknowledge and send love to all persons I meet today. The twin symbol for the number one is a circle.

Two represents a growing desire to satisfy the unfinished business of the soul. There is still past actions (Karma) yet to be addressed and therefore balanced. It is the ying and yang; hot and cold; left and right; light and dark; male and female. These individuals must seek out all the opposites contrary to their current beliefs and seek the center. A prayer for this number:

Holy Father, I pray to bring understanding to all thoughts, actions and emotions that reflect the opposite of my current beliefs.

Three represents the holy trinity. Like the number seven, this number is a spiritual calling requiring that one seek a higher level of consciousness to see the universal plan. One must challenge all beliefs that do not unify.

Q- I always considered the number 3 a creative number?

SG- Yes, the trinity is all there is in creation.

Holy Father, I accept my symbolic place as a spirit and ask for the balance the number three requires of me. The matching graphic is a triangle.

Four- This soul has chosen to become part of the organization of others with the goal of assisting those who are out of balance. This is the number of the group. The focus is on the mind. The person with this birth number is a clear thinker and a leader. The four may forget its greater purpose, as the physical world is more attractive than the spiritual. The number four wants to see and be seen. They will have a difficult time seeing themselves first as spirit. Fewer souls born under the number 4 will come to see you for assistance as they have difficulty understanding mediumship.

I answered that this has been true.

SG- *Holy Father, we ask that all souls born with the physical energy of the four break this even number into pieces so they may clearly see themselves as spirit. The graphic symbol is a square.*

Five- A soul born with 5 energy can miss-use it if not very careful. This soul has been deprived in other lives and has chosen a number with a high vibration. This is a physical number because of the energy of the group. The five soul does not work well in a solo environment and requires others. In this respect, the soul imprinted with this number exerts more physical energy. He or she must balance numerous activities, and in the process include many other people. The five also needs balance in the physical world. Its graphic is a crystalline pentagram and although it provides immense physical support, it can cloud the soul's ability to balance and reach into the unseen world. The number 5 is not an easy number to live with.

Holy Father, we pray that limits of action be placed upon the heart of this person. Direct them to the peace which can be found in isolation and solace. Bless and protect the body of the number five as they do too much.

Six is a warm and nurturing soul. The soul needs comfort and tends to be drawn towards the physical, rather than spiritual. It is, however, a strong number and can lead in the right direction which is toward spiritual wisdom. The number 6 must understand when caring for others that there is a deeper connection beyond the care of the body. It is the number associated with many health care providers.

Holy Father, bless the souls with the gift of the number 6. Pray that this strong birth energy be transformed into a higher level of understanding of one's role in the greater world of spirit.

Seven represents that which cannot be seen but is active in one's life. It is the unseen forces that are present. This is the seeker who feels connected to spirit and cannot deny the bigger picture of what really exists. To deny it will create tension and one must return over and over to the cosmic blue-print.

Holy Father, open up all the channels to those born with the number 7 and willing to assist others in a spiritual way. Bless them with great love and peace and bring those souls who seek comfort to their thresholds. Amen

Eight is the most physical birth number and requires stability in the material world. Those who strive to be successful in a material way may neglect their soul.

Holy Father, remind me that my soul is my focus. In caring for the invisible part of me, the material substance will be provided. Remember that the real treasure is the spirit.

Nine is a strong birth number. Those born with a nine, walk the path of serving others. When the number nine is paired with the number seven, a powerful union can be created. Many of these souls create change in the seen world which affects souls later as they grow toward the unseen realms.

Eleven is considered a master number. It is a double digit number in which the power of the one is multiplied. A strong personality is led to a higher level of action through-out the life-time. This person is actively engaged in helping others and may begin new organizations to do so. It is a call to be very "awake." It is an action number.

Q- Are there negative aspects of particular numbers?

SG- The positive energies of a particular number can be reversed by those who choose to throw it away. The reversal is always possible as all possess free will.

Q- What about number sequences. How do we interpret them?

SG- Number sequences also carry messages.

Q- What is most important, the first or last number in the sequence?

SG- The two outer numbers support the center number.

Q- I gave him the number 471 to interpret

SG- There are physical things needed to open up spiritual doors.

Q- What about 2 numbers?

SG- The first number is the lead and holds the energy. So in 51, the 5 will lead you to 1. Many tasks will bring focus to the central issue.

Exercise

List your birth number followed by five symbols that have meaning to you. These symbols will be physical objects and next to them list the spiritual meaning.

For example, my birth number is a #7 and my five objects/shapes would be the following:

The circle – This is a sacred shape as evidenced by the Mandala.

A paintbrush – This allows me to express my intuition which flows from my soul.

The Book- *The Course in Miracles*- a holy book which reminds me that I am connected to everyone I see.

Saint Brigid's Cross- Connects me to prayer and my love of Ireland.

A rose quartz crystal – a symbol of love.

Soul Colors

Q-What about colors? Do they have meaning?

SG–Colors are significant.

Yellow is the color of knowledge and education. It represents everlasting light and understanding. Clarification of thoughts – softness and peace. Yellow represents clear thinking and clear speaking. Yellow souls are seeking answers to questions throughout their lives in physical bodies.

Red is the color of power and may get souls into trouble. The miss use of red is seen in the world today. A red soul may, however, be called toward a higher level of action

Q- What about Hitler?

SG- He was a red soul without the supporting colors.

Q-Tell me more about supporting colors?

SG-Soul colors are always a mixture – you are a blue soul with violet and yellow tints.

Blue is the color of harmony and love. The color of those on a high spiritual path. The violet is your connection with those of us here and yellow represents the love of learning.

I asked him to comment on my husband Don?

SG-Don is a green soul with red and blue. A green soul loves the earth and the presence of this soul brings healing to others. Green souls are close to the earth that they choose professions that allow them to be outdoors. They are free spirits and do not like to be controlled. The red is power and he carries this energy in the correct amount. Blue is the spiritual color and connects him to the spiritual realm.

Q- So colors can change?

SG- Yes they change throughout one's life.

Q-W hat about white?

SG- **White** is no color and can be a problem with new souls. White always is accompanied by other bits of color. In a new soul this is the case because there has been little life experience.

Q-What about black?

SG-**Black** is many colors blended together and has often been given a bad reputation. Just as there must be light-- darkness must follow. So black can be a soul who had a greater density of color than most – a soul who has been overwhelmed with all the hues. Do you understand?

I answered that I did not completely understand.

SG-Black indicates an embodied soul who is spiritually, and often physically not well. It is not uncommon to have a bit of other colors included, but when there is more of the black, a soul is in need of help and there are many guides involved.

Q-I mentioned a number of world leaders from the past and asked him if they were the color black. I was thinking of Mussolini and Genghis Khan?

SG-Many of these leaders you mentioned were partially black and were a strong combination of red and black resulting in confusion, dementia, lack of interest in love and those other beings in the environment.

We continued with the colors.

SG-**Violet** represents the connection to spirit and the larger the amount of violet, the closer to us here. The violet in your aura grows rapidly as you work with us to help others.

Orange-This is the color which sits between yellow and red. So usually belongs with a younger soul who seeks more involvement with the physical dimension. This is a soul seeking knowledge but autonomy as well. Orange souls are often carrying bits of green, yellow and brown.

Pink – is a diluted version of red. Pink souls may appear to be powerful, but they are really not. They are often young souls. Pink is often included in those that are almost completely white. Pink is like an actor trying out the world but not sure what is next.

Brown – is a mixture of green and blue and it is the color of confusion. Brown souls, like black souls, are being restrained from the true understanding of their path.

Soul Names

Q-A few years ago when my husband Don had a between lives session he was given a soul name of Jonaseth. I was told that each person has a soul name. Is this true?

SG-The name follows each soul in the life-time and its sound which resonates as it is heard, or others speak it is powerful. The soul name is a constant and resonates underneath the birth name. It is permanent. The birth name is temporary and is only associated with one life-time.

Q- What happens if someone rejects their birth name?

SG- When this happens it is a rejection of the parent's initial instincts. The parent is prompted to choose the name. The soul, however, desires a different energy and asserts his/her independence. This is often a younger soul.

Q- When should somebody know their soul name?

SG- It is not time for young souls to know it. They ride it quietly through life. It is like a sled as they glide through life. For others it is revealed when they take on the healing of others. This is true for you.

Q-My soul name is Ramalerin and I asked how to bring it into my life?

SG- Speak it often, write it, become aware of the energy of the name and begin to wear it like a warm robe. Try it out as it is an old friend.

Q- I asked Saint Germain to comment on particular birth names and the meanings but it became clear to me that this is a massive amount of material that I will save for another book. The name given to you by your parents is special and is a significant symbol that you carry with you every day. Its sound is a vibration that also has meaning.

SG- The energy of the birth canal is an imprint on the soul. One comes into the world with a road map to the life ahead.

Other Symbols

The Cross

Q- Can you define the meaning of the cross?

SG- This is a general discourse that may relate to all crosses. The center is the love of God—the universal consciousness. The vertical board is the representation of the higher spiritual realms intersecting the horizontal line of this physical world. All connected by the center. The circle often seen on the Celtic cross is the greater connection to everything.

Q- Please talk about some other symbols?

He brought my attention to the objects on my desk and pointed out that they have meanings. My candle, he says, represents the light. Seeing in the dark. Waking up to what is true. Focus on one part of the flame and burn up what is no longer necessary. Choose an issue and bring it to the candle. Write down your thoughts.

SG We ask you to consider the symbols – to meditate on these and see how they are connected to your life in ways other than your physical endeavors.

Exercise:

List 5 symbols that have meaning for you and discern their meanings. Remember that the symbol is personal for you.

CIRCLES- MANDALAS

"As we form the circle of love for each other, we also unite our energetic connection with all other beings on the planet. We acknowledge the power of the connection we have made both symbolically and energetically. We pray for those in our personal circles and for the greater good of the planet in the universe. We do not in any way think that this is not one of the most powerful actions we perform as a group. And so we bless the world and use the energetic circle to create love."- Saint Germain

The circle represents the light of the world and the connection to all. The symbol is the most powerful of the universal symbols. The

70

shape of one's head is a circle. The planetary bodies are circles. A ball is a circle which unites all who play with it. Circles form in the oceans and on the sand. We can heal the planet with this simple shape. When a group of individuals form the human circle they bring energy and universal power to a place, and this is an energetic healing. So, the prayer circle is an energetic vortex, reaching to the upper worlds. It is like a funnel of energy.

An exercise in creating circles

Don't feel as if you have to be an artist to do this exercise. Just do it intuitively by expressing the first thing that comes to your mind. Draw the circle and then let the other shapes emerge and form. I have included two of my own illustrations as an example of how simple this can be.

SG- Create a circle associated with all of these different words. Each one will be a page of writing and drawing. Your written words must contain at least one of the following four words:

Circle   .

Art

Broken love

Continuity

The drawing of the circle must represent the word either abstractly or in real terms.

Myself

My family

Unconditional love

Friends

Work

Time alone

My activities

Helping others

Connection to all there is

God

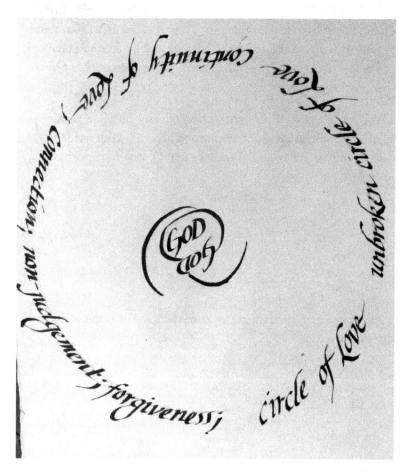

GOD

Love; Love; Love and connection; Love and connection; Love and connection; Love and connection; Love and connection;

lack of forgiveness

Forgiveness

FORGIVENESS

73

CHAPTER 9
DEATH
BETWEEN LIVES. PAST LIVES

Between Lives

Q- What happens the moment we die?

SG- One will experience and create what it desires on the spirit side. Death is easier than birth. Once the soul leaves his/her body they are assisted to move on to a level best suited to their level of understanding and where the soul can continue to grow. If food is desired it will be available. The soul creates reality instantly. In your current earth-bound location the same is true; however the denser energy of the body restricts the instant gratification of one's thoughts.

Q- Where is the location of the spirit world? I understand from a previous conversation that energetically spirit is at a higher vibration, but that it is in the same space as us?

SG-Yes, this is correct. The space is superimposed upon the physical plane, but only those like you can see it. Spirit is energy and does not take up space. It is, therefore, not moving upward but remains in the layers where it was embodied. Do you understand?

Q-This is a difficult concept. Does one just drop the body and the energy is still present?

SG-The energy remains close to the body for at least the number of days it takes to dispose of the body. The support team assigned to the soul accompanies them to the realm where they will be instructed to review the past life experience. This is not a place, but a dimension of space close to you vibrationally.

Q- Is there a lower astral level where pain and suffering take place?

SG- Yes. Those who live a poor life with little love and compassion for others may end up in the lower astral realm. However, remorse for poor decisions affecting others adversely, will bring a soul to the level where others are ready to serve their spiritual needs and move them ahead.

Note- It is not necessary for souls to remain in the lower astral levels if they are ready to acknowledge poor behavior and make amends.

Q- Why is it not possible for everyone to be a medium and communicate with loved ones who are in spirit?

SG- Only an old soul having lived many lives can listen to those who have entered their spirit body.

Q- How does the one in spirit who has no mind or brain hear us on this side?

SG- The soul has a communication system without words—a channel/medium is like a beacon in the spirit world and both can hear. Connecting with one's loved ones is a combination of many factors. There are moments when the channels open wider than at other times. If a soul is very concerned and energetically powerful and wants to get the message through it is easier to hear. The more one communicates with spirit, the greater the ability becomes. One must overlook nothing when tuning in to the spirit world.

Q-Do those in spirit check in with their loved ones? How strong is the connection, and can we see the intimate details of their lives?

SG-Yes, they are taught this skill very quickly and can do this without fear or sadness. They may have as much contact as desired. No communication is restricted, however, very few souls choose to see the lives of their families continuing on in the physical realm. Life is busy and challenging here in the spiritual world. There is work for all, particularly in assisting souls who must adjust after physical death. Once one steps over the threshold between physical and spiritual worlds, events of the physical world are pale in comparison to the enticement offered here.

Q- During a previous conversation with St. Germain he mentioned that we are participating in a classroom on the other side when we are in the dream state. I asked him to talk to me more about this education that takes place when we are between lives?

SG – The spiritual world is a large classroom and it prepares you for the road ahead. So, there are classes here. One chooses a curriculum designed by you and your Council of Elders. During the physical experience it is necessary to continue with the previous curriculum in order to have what you might say, is a refresher course. Therefore, all physical beings are encouraged to come back for more instruction during their dreams.

Q- So nobody is forced into this education?

SG-There is no force, only strong encouragement from one's guide. To delay the instruction is to hold oneself back on the path to a greater understanding.

Past Lives

The soul is like a spool of thread. As it grows through experiences in every physical life, it either earns more thread or takes some away. In this way it expands its knowledge. The threads of each life are chosen by the soul. There is no force of any kind in the choosing. Help and guidance are offered but there are never demands. All is an individual choice. - Saint Germain

This is a subject of great interest to me. I have experienced two past life regressions and remembered a few more past lives through dreams. Saint Germain asked me if the subject appealed to me and I gave him a strong affirmative yes.

SG- The human body makes its way through numerous incarnations in the physical world. All genders and races must be experienced in a path to wholeness of spirit. Those who remember these physical experiences while in their bodies have a more rapid ascension. Being UN aware of the law of re-birth is a dis-advantage and slows one down. Do you have any questions?

Q- Yes- how can people connect with these past lives?

Yeshua (Jesus) - Dear heart you may assist others, whenever the opportunity comes to share this information. Each soul remembers, on some level of their being, and some cannot ignore the sense of doing or being in a place they have been before. Others are so caught up in the world of flesh they do not receive the signs.

Q- I made reference to my two sisters and how different their understanding was on this subject.

Yeshua (Jesus) - We know these souls you love. Both have had lives with you. One remembers clearly. The other has not lived in the physical world long enough to be ready.

He went on to tell me my family was a mix of young and old souls and I was placed in the family to raise their spiritual understanding.

Please listen to the past-life meditation on www.artspeakstosoul.com under videos.

Q- When one crosses over to the other side and begins to make decisions about the next life it must be a huge decision. How does this process work? What happens when we die?

SG – The soul steps very quickly into their spiritual body you might say, and as they do, they exist on the level of welcoming, which you may call the first astral plane. This term astral is designed by you and not used here. The soul is welcomed and greeted by the loved ones – both past and present. So all souls connect with loved ones from every physical incarnation in the body. The reunion is a happy occasion. All ill or negative thoughts are absent at that moment. The soul is taken by their guides or angels to a place of comfort and one that is reminiscent of previous surroundings. On this level they learn about communication with their loved ones still embodied and instructed about the plan for them while in spirit. Once the reunion and debriefing has been completed, the soul is taken to a place of rest. This is often determined by the manner of death. One who leaves the body in a traumatic situation is allowed to rest a long time. Those with natural deaths rest quietly for a moment in comparison, and then meet their Council of Elders to have the life review. This review is complete and includes all events of the previous life. This process is gentle and handled with great care by the elders. The goal is to instruct. Most souls are humble when faced with the emotions associated with their actions in the body.

They are then taken to their soul group. All are aligned with a group of like – minded, spiritually matched energies and this is where different levels are indicated. Undisciplined energies are able to re – invent the physical experience as a way of practicing the last life. There is the ability to repeat an action more than one time and experience a variety of consequences. Other souls rise to a level of study, and spend time learning to help others and to activate the spiritual gifts. This was your last stop here in the spiritual world.

Q- Can we see what would have happened differently in our physical lives when we view these events while in spirit?

Yeshua (Jesus) - Yes, this is part of the divine classroom. Every action, however small, can be seen and re-lived again and again in numerous ways. Only this replay and re-wind will teach you not to repeat previous mistakes. Some souls replay life events thousands of times; other are not interested in the lesson.

Q- How do you practice your spiritual gifts in the spiritual world?

SG – By working with other souls who send you messages, visions, and feelings. It is a team effort.

Q- Is this the highest level?

SG – This is one of many high places as you put it. There is the highest level where one becomes a spiritual servant for others. This involves the willingness to guide a soul who is embodied. You will be offered the decision to stay here and work from this realm, or to re-enter the body again to work with us on the planet. Careful study is necessary just like a class on a college campus with books and homework. There are classes and late-night studies. One must first show complete understanding of how love was and was not practiced while in the physical body. Once this is firmly established, planning the next life can take place.

Q- How many choices are there?

SG- As many choices as the soul wants to consider. Some consider 1000 possibilities and play with them for a long time—others make decisions quickly and are anxious to resume the physical experience.

Q- Could you be more specific about the process?

SG- Each returning soul has an outline of the chapters of their life. This is not the Akashic record but is instead a small text associated with a singular life experience in the body. Each chapter contains a certain number of earth years.

Note – The Akashic Record contains the information about all our previous lives. It is often depicted as a book. When I conduct a reading for someone, I am often shown their book. We are offered the opportunity to read and study it when we leave the physical world and return to our natural state as spirits.

Q- Is the time of death or the number of earth years pre-planned?

SG- No, not exactly. There is, however, a general consensus from the members of your council as to the length of the new life. And so, within each chapter you are guided to follow the story with the help of guides and angels by your side. They have learned to influence you in ways that will re-direct you if necessary.

Q- What if one gets off track?

SG- That may occur in the case of unforeseen accidents and then we start over. The life's chapters are, however, carefully overseen.

Q- It sounds very rigid?

SG- Yes, carefully planned and with obstacles as well. Only difficulties and uncomfortable moments can achieve the highest potential of the soul. Do you see?

I answered yes and he continued to say,

SG- Each chapter is at least a decade of years with a heading and below that a calendar of events each year. The calendar is the part of the plan subject to change-yet, it is carefully monitored as well. Days are part of the calendar cycle and we watch and nudge gently as you go through your regular activities.

Q- Most people don't know this.

SG- Your own guide has good and frustrating days with you.

We talked a while longer about how carefully choreographed this is. I found the information very interesting. I was aware there was a plan for our physical life, but had no idea of the level of detail involved.

SG- Do not be self- conscious about this as you go about your daily life. The veil is not intrusive.

Q – What about war? I have heard that soldiers return to the body quickly?

SG- Yes, you are correct. The desire to return quickly is based upon re-uniting with loved ones. In any traumatic life event this quick turn-around is often desired. There is senior counsel against this, but no pressure is ever brought.

Q- What about 9-11 and the souls who lost their lives?

SG- Half of those souls have already been re-born into a body.

Q- How can one remember a past life?

SG- Remembrance of all lives comes when the soul is ready. Dreams will lead the way first.

CHAPTER 10

DREAMS

"Place your thoughts on the table before going to sleep and ask these thoughts to speak to you in the dream state while the body is left behind."

Dreams are a source of powerful information. I believe that they are either telling us about our current situation, or showing us a past experience that is affecting us at the moment.

In 2005 I had a dream which lasted five nights. It was a lucid dream which means I was able to hear, see, and feel, and speak in the dream. Every morning I wrote the information down until the 6th night when nothing happened. I had so much material including street names and places that I was able to find the town and street on Google World where I lived in 18th century England.

At the time of the dream I was in a bad marriage with a controlling partner. The dream was showing me a past life with the same man. I confirmed this dream and gained additional information through a past life regression. Ultimately I left the relationship and I believe the dream helped me to see my situation more clearly, and move on past the relationship.

I asked Saint Germain to speak to me about dreams, Déjà vu and alternate realities.

Q- Why are there times when we cannot remember our dreams?

SG- There are times when it is better to have the unconscious understanding and then later the conscious material will emerge.

Q- What is an alternate reality or déjà vu?

SG- An alternate reality is a form of altered consciousness in which a person is momentarily put into a remarkable state of remembering a past event. This happens frequently, but not many are aware when it occurs.

Q- When this occurs is there anything to be gained?

SG- This is a good question. There is often a message in this event but the experience is so fleeting, one can often miss the message.

I expressed my difficulty in understanding the whole issue of time and alternate realities. He replied, Time is nothing. All happens at the same time, and as you know, it is only a man-made construct.

Q- What about other lives—are they happening at the same time?

SG – Yes, all simultaneously.

Q- Does this only pertain to the earth?

SG- No-all happens at once. The material plane is constantly changing which is why you refer to it as an illusion.

Q- Do time lines shift?

SG- Yes, this may occur but in very small bits so as not to upset the current timeline or confuse the individual

Q-What about out of body experiences?

SG- These you experience many times in your sleep and most are not remembered. You do, however, gain insight and knowledge when in this state of consciousness. It is healing and regenerative. It is necessary for good health.

Q – I cannot remember all my out of body experiences?

SG – These are not meant to be remembered each time. Quiet work by spirit is accomplished in the sleep state and not everyone needs to recognize that they are having this experience

Q- Do we always leave our bodies at night?

SG- Almost all souls do this naturally. To be encased or restricted in the body is unhealthy. It is imperative that the soul leave in order to return to their real home and continue with their educations.

Note-   Saint Germain explained to me that we are educated in our dreams. We return to the spiritual classroom and the studies we were engaged in previously while in our spirit bodies.

Q- I expressed concern about those people unable to dream.

 SG- People who are afraid are the ones who do not sleep well. They purposely avoid the travel so important to their soul's growth.

Exercise: Assistance for those who cannot dream.

Write a letter with a list of all things you need assistance with. It will be answered in some way within a short period of time. Be observant of the (signs) that are sent to you. Your guides will respond.

Note- When we write down our personal goals for our daily life we should pray for guidance in meeting them.

CHAPTER 11
LIFE ON OTHER WORLDS

Q-I have always been fascinated with the possibility of life on other planets.

Q- Are there other civilizations and planets with conscious beings living there?

SG- There are living beings in thousands of planetary bodies. Some are very advanced and able to instantly travel to other worlds. Some suffer from some of the same problems we have here on earth. Earth has and will continue to be visited by other beings. This is not an issue to create fear. Extraterrestrial beings capable of reaching the other planetary systems are far advanced in technology and spirituality. Most of these beings are far more enlightened than those on planet Earth. Earth is young and one of the most difficult planets to practice harmony.

Q- I asked if our leaders have had contact with these beings.

SG- Visitation has been long standing over centuries. The current world's view is to protect people from this knowledge. This is a fear- based view. In the years ahead this will be modified when new leaders review past records. The United States and Russia have gained from the interaction with these extraterrestrials and the information is held in secret by a very small group of individuals.

Q- Does the president of the United States know this?

SG- Yes, all America's Presidents have kept the secret.

Q- I've heard about beings called the Elohim. I had been previously told that I was a star being and wondered if the origins of life were somehow attached to the Elohim?

SG- The origin of your soul was from a star system very far away and much further than the Elohim. He spelled the name of the star system and told me the place was one of great love and souls coming from it were very blessed. It is a place where the body is very different. It is primarily light energy with a small amount of physical matter. He told me that the star system is so many light years away from the earth's current location it has not ever been discovered by scientists here on earth.

Q-Are there many star beings from other planets here on earth now?

SG- Yes there are many here and I knew some of them.

CHAPTER 12

Saint Germain and the Violet Flame.

During one of my early channeling sessions with St. Germain I asked him how he would like me to describe him to the readers of this book, as so many books and articles have been written about him. This was his response.

SG – More has been written than has been necessary. As you know, I have had many earth incarnations. All prepared me for what I do in spirit. This is to work with messengers such as you to bring healing to those that will listen. Many do not, and this brings pain and heartache to those of us in spirit. I am a master of spiritual knowledge and the keeper of the Violet flame.

Jane – I asked St. Germain if he would comment on the Violet Flame.

SG – The Violet Flame burns without ceasing. The flame represents the power of the universal mind and the energetic harmony of all souls. To step into the flame is the greatest experience of mankind. It is a gift to mankind, but very few are aware of its power and availability. It will alter the energy of those who use it wisely. It is not a toy or a passing fancy but a serious energy for those who may be ready to work with and within it.

I personally have stepped into the Violet flame and much to my surprise it was actually a cool flame rather than hot. It was part of my initiation as one of his messengers. This was a deeply moving experience for me. I believe that following the experience my energy rose to a higher level of spiritual understanding.

St. Germain was also involved with our founding fathers here in America. When asked about this he made the following comment,

SG- The founding fathers were connected to me and other spiritual masters in a time of great turmoil, however, this was a time of major expansion of thinking and thought for those on the earthly plane.

Q- Were you present during the signing of the declaration of independence as is often mentioned?

SG- Yes, I was a voice channel for Thomas Jefferson.

There are many books written about St. Germain and some of his lives have been as Samuel the Prophet of the Old Testament, Christopher Columbus, Claude Louis, Comte de Saint Germain, St. Joseph the father of Jesus, and Sir Francis Bacon to name only a few. For more information about him and his many lives please visit www of .artspeakstosoul.com.

CHAPTER 14

FINAL WORDS

SG- This is a workbook of love and understanding. A path to a higher understanding of who you are through your connection to all other persons and situations during this experience in the physical dimension. As in all workbooks, one must be diligent in completing the work. The discipline required will lead you to experience your physical world with a better understanding of why you are here. Note that the basic truths contained in my messages are meant to expand your path upwards to a level which opens many doors for you. These doors open both in the world of physical form and the spiritual realm.

Do not take this work lightly. Your guides will assist you if you have difficulty. This book requires only a moment each day in order to gain a greater level of wisdom. And so, we conclude with the issues of deepest concern for all who recognize their worth as spirit, and not as a body.

Love is all there is and the most magnificent gift you give to all other persons including yourself. This gift is never discarded, but carried with the soul through all incarnations. Hate is the only barrier to losing it. Love yourself and all others in knowing you are spirit, not body. Do not carry burdens of pain and remorse. Live this moment to it's fullest in love and grace.

Remember that you will experience many more incarnations in the body. Relax and do not rush through each moment in fear that it will be your last. Spend a moment of silence first thing in the morning and embrace the sunrise.

Love all other persons, animals, and the natural world. Take care of your planet. Treat your body with love. Treat it well and do not cloud the energy field with substances that block the highest vibration of spirit from reaching you. Love each person and forgive all things. Be at peace. Prepare for new spiritual wisdom as you begin to walk the path of love. Remember that you are never alone. The guidance provided to each soul is deeply revealed and present every moment of the day. Be open and watchful for all instances of connection with your spiritual helpers.

Live in love, work in love, and send love to all you meet. Carry love wherever you go. Bless all beings and look toward the higher realms of consciousness. You are beautiful and loved by us here. Keep this prayer close:

Holy Father, I am remembering that I am a Holy Spirit and everyone I see is pure love.

Dear hearts we commend you for reading and practicing the lessons of this book. You are surrounded with love and wisdom from the spiritual dimensions. Know that we are pleased and present in your energetic fields. Love is sent to you as a ball of light. Realize that every time you send love messages to others they bounce back to you. Bless and keep you in the Holy Spirit of knowing you are loved and are love. Amen

Archangel Raphael- the healing energies of the Angels are sent to you and those who embrace these words. God bless you and this book of love.

Archangel Chamuel- I bless you with the peace which comes from knowing you are unlimited and protected. Deep peace is sent to you and blessings from the angels of compassion and forgiveness.

St. Brigid – I hold you in my arms and bless you with quiet grace. God grant you the desire and ability to pass this on to all who meet. The holiness surrounds those who understand the deep meaning of life in spirit. Amen.

PRAYERS, MEDITATION, AND SILENCE

A prayer to start the day

SG- Take one moment early in the day and devote it to reconnection of soul with spirit.

Holy Father I am your representative in the flesh. Let me set an example you all others as all I need is love and light.

SILENCE

St. Brigid of Ireland speaks about silence. "Silence is powerful and more than anything else in your world the body needs it for centering and abiding peace. This silence is total absence of sound. There is nothing to do, nothing to ponder, only quiet and peace. The practice of silence was a daily course in my soul sojourn on the earth. Every morning when you wake, sit in silence for a short time and gradually nothingness. This discipline will give your body and mind the kindness of spirit you desire. This is recommended for all souls within the dense energy of the body and physical world."

Q- Are the sounds or the music associated with most meditation not ideal?

Saint Brigid- No, they are baby steps to the most powerful practice which is total silence. Sounds are not necessary for peace.

I responded that I had often participated in meditations with sound – not only musical sounds but also the sound of a voice and it was extremely relaxing and provided a feeling of peace. Saint

Brigid- Yes, but the relaxation experience is temporary. Practice of silence yields permanent results and will assist you in spiritual work.

Closing Prayer

Deep love and gratitude to those of you who have read and studied the pages of this workbook. One will experience the effect of these efforts in the days ahead. Dear Father, we bless these souls who desire the connection with their greater self – spirit which supports all life and thought in the physical world. Take these lovely souls to a greater understanding of their purpose here, and work with them. Assist all who make the effort to reconnect with their soul. All assistance is available at any moment at one's request. Blessings and love from my soul to yours. - Saint Germain

Jane Halliwell Green is a messenger of the Ascended Master St. Germain. She can be reached at

http://www.artspeakstosoul.com

jane@artspeakstosoul.com

jane@janehalliwell.com

CPSIA information can be obtained
at www.ICGtesting.com
Printed in the USA
LVHW081433260121
677545LV00041B/1875

9 780615 987170